Saracenic Architecture

William Robert Ware

In the interest of creating a more extensive selection of rare historical book reprints, we have chosen to reproduce this title even though it may possibly have occasional imperfections such as missing and blurred pages, missing text, poor pictures, markings, dark backgrounds and other reproduction issues beyond our control. Because this work is culturally important, we have made it available as a part of our commitment to protecting, preserving and promoting the world's literature. Thank you for your understanding.

PLATE I.

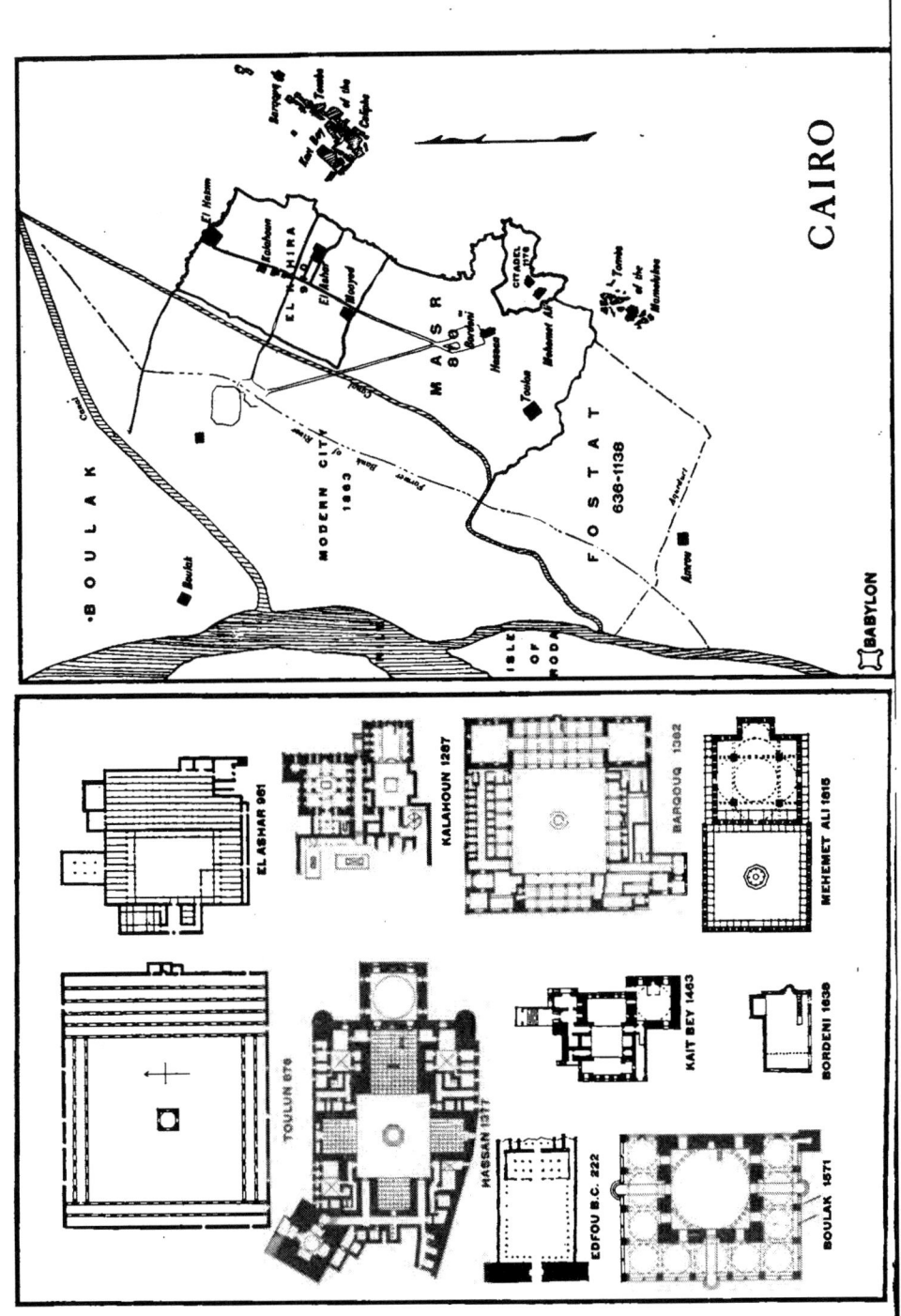

HISTORICAL TABLE.

622 Hegira	632 MAHOMET dies
"The Four First CALIPHS" (Successors)	at Medina (30 years)
632 ABU BEKR, father-in-law	634 OMAR, general
644 OTHMAN, general (Ommiad)	656 ALI, son-in-law (Fatima)
	(Abbas, uncle)

EGYPT	662 OMMIAD CALIPHS
638 Amrou conquers Egypt	Damascus (90 years)
Mosque at Fostat, 642	Mosques at Jerusalem, 637, 691
	Mosque at Damascus, 705
	700 Musa conquers Africa
	711 Tarik, Battle of Xeres
	"Roderick, the last of the Goths"
	732 Charles Martel, Battle of Tours
	750 OMMIAD CALIPHS
	Cordova (500 years)

750 *Abbassides*	750 ABBASSIDE CALIPHS
(120 years)	Bagdad (500 years)
870 *Toulonides* (Turcoman mercenaries)	810 Haroun-al-Raschid
Mosque of Toulun, 876.	Tombs at Bagdad
970 *Fatimites* (El Moezz)	
(200 years)	
Cairo	
Mosque El Ashar, 981	
Mosque El Hakim, 1000	
1170 *Ayoubites* (Saladin, Seljukian)	1055 Seljukian Turks take Bagdad
(80 years)	1075 Seljukians take Iconium
Citadel	1096 Seljukians take Damascus
Mameluke Sultans	
1250 *Baharites* (Turkish slaves)	1250 Mongols conquer Bagdad
(132 years)	1299 Ottoman Turks take Iconium
Mosque of Kalahoun, 1287	Mosques at Broussa, 1389
Mosque of Hassan, 1377	
1382 *Borghites* (Circassian slaves)	
(135 years)	
Mosque of Barqouq, 1382	
Mosque of Moayed, 1412	
Mosque of Kait Bey, 1463	1453 Ottomans take Constantinople

1517 Osman Selim conquers Egypt	1453 TURKISH CALIPHS
Mameluke Governors	Sulimanieh Mosque, 1550
(300 years)	Validé Mosque, 1665
Mosque at Boulak, 1571	Laleli Mosque, 1760
Bordeni Mosque, 1638	
1806 *Mehemet Ali*	
Mosque in Citadel, 1815.	

acc. no. 1164
Gift of Mr. Forbes
Feb. 16, 1917

NOTE.

The Historical Table prefixed to this paper gives at tne top the date of the Hegira, of the death of Mahomet, and of the accession of the "Four First Caliphs" who succeeded him at Medina.

Below are given the names and dates of the successive dynasties which have held sway in Egypt from that time to this, in nominal subjection to the Ommiad, Abbasside, and Turkish Caliphs, who have inherited, or assumed, the spiritual authority of the founders. The table contains the names of the principal sultans and of the more important of the Cairo mosques and their plans are given, and their position in the city shown, in Plate I.

In a second column are given the principal contemporaneous events of Mohammedan history outside of Egypt, so far, at least, as they concern the immediate object of this paper. It marks the duration of the Ommiad, Abbasside, and Turkish caliphates.

HARVARD ENGINEERING JOURNAL

Devoted to the interests of Engineering
and Architecture at Harvard University

VOL. IV APRIL, 1905 NO. 1

SARACENIC ARCHITECTURE.

By Professor William R. Ware, '52.

I.

MAHOMET was an Arab chief, and the Arabs were barbarous tribes of the desert with no art, and no materials for art, except for the art of poetry. Painting, sculpture and architecture were alike unknown to them. In Egypt they came in contact with the Byzantine Empire, and with what remained of the civilization of the Roman Empire and of the Greek Empire of Alexander, and, what was more important, with what remained of the old Egyptian civilization, an influence which already had produced marked effects not only upon the Romans and the Greeks, but upon the Jewish colonists who had settled in Alexandria. Meanwhile the peculiarly mystical turn of the Egyptian mind had affected both philosophy and religion, and to this day it affects the philosophy and religion of all Christian countries.

The Hegira, or flight of Mahomet from Mecca to Medina, took place in the year 622, and he died in 632, ten years later. The first Caliphs, the successors, of Mahomet, were his father-in-law, Abu Bekr, his generals, Omar and Othman, and his son-in-law, Ali. They are known in history as the Four First Caliphs.

NOTE.— The substance of this paper is taken from a lecture given at the Metropolitan Museum, in New York, in February, 1899, and again in Cambridge, before the *Pen and Brush Club*, in March, 1904.

Some of the figures in Plates XI and XII are taken from M. Gayet's "*Art Arabe*," a volume to which I am indebted also for much information. The rest are taken mostly from photographs, and from sketches made in Egypt and Asia Minor in 1890.

They established and maintained the caliphate at Medina for thirty years. It was the caliph Omar who, with his General Amrou, conquered Egypt and burned the Alexandrian library, or is said to have done so; the next, Othman, belonged to the Ommiad family, of Medina. The fourth caliph was Ali, the husband of Mahomet's only child Fatima, and the disputes which followed his accession have divided the Mohammedan world to this day between the Sunnites, or orthodox Mohammedans, and the Shiites, or Fatimites, the followers of Ali. The Shiites, though adhering to the only descendants of the prophet, are held to be heretics and dissenters.

At the end of the thirty years, that is to say in the year 662, the Ommiads, of the family of Othman, murdered Ali and his two sons Hassan and Hussein, and removed the caliphate to Damascus, where it remained for ninety years. It is rather singular that although Hassan and Hussein belonged to the hated sect of the Shiites, they are held in the greatest veneration by the orthodox Sunnites. They are the most revered of Mohammedan saints and martyrs, and the day of their death is everywhere celebrated with tumultuous demonstrations of grief. Even in London, the Mohammedan sailors make the docks resound with their lamentations. The martyrs Hassan and Hussein are known in Cairo as the Hosaneyn. By the unbelieving inhabitants of East London, they are called Hobson and Jobson.

In 750, the descendants of Mahomet's uncle, Abbas, came to the front, and in their turn murdered at Damascus all the Ommiads but two. One of these escaped to Southern Arabia, where he founded an Ommiad Caliphate which lasted 800 years. The other, Abd-er-Rahman, a little boy, fled to Spain and founded the caliphate of Cordova. At the same time the Abbassides moved the orthodox caliphate from Damascus to Bagdad, where they reigned for five hundred years until, in 1250, they were conquered by the Mongols, or Moguls, and took refuge in Cairo, where the caliphate remained until the sixteenth century, when the Turks took possession and carried it to Constantinople.

Meanwhile Musa, a Mohammedan general of the Ommiads, conquered the north of Africa. This conquest is about the only important event with which to mark the year 700. In 711, Tarik crossed the Straits of Gibraltar, which takes its name from him, Gebel-el-Tarik, the Hill of Tarik, and conquered Roderick, "the Last of the Goths," in the battle of Xeres. In 732, spreading into France, just a century after the death of Mahomet, the Arabs were defeated by Charles Martel in the battle of Tours. Thus, it is held, was France, and in fact the whole of Europe, rescued from Mohammedan control and perhaps from the Mohammedan religion.

Finally, the Turks, in two bodies, seized Syria and Asia Minor. The Seljukian Turks who maintained themselves at Iconium in Lycaonia during the twelfth and thirteenth centuries, were followed at the beginning of the fourteenth century by the Ottoman Turks, who established their capital at Broussa in Bithynia, fifty or sixty miles south of Constantinople. They took Constantinople in 1453, and fifty years later conquered Egypt, and the Turkish Sultan assumed the title of caliph. The principal monuments of the Turks are their mosques at Constantinople.

We will here consider only the Mohammedan architecture which has the best claim to be called Saracenic, that of Egypt. It was not only the earliest, but, being the first, it gave tone and character to the architecture of every country which the Mohammedans conquered. Everything in Spain, Persia and even India seems to have obtained its main inspiration from the architecture of Egypt.

In the year 638 Amrou, the general of the caliph Omar, conquered Egypt, and in 642 founded a town near the old Roman fortress called Babylon, which stood on the eastern bank of the Nile, just below Memphis, at the head of the Delta. He then proceeded to the conquest of Alexandria, but as he was striking his tent, he noticed that a couple of doves were building their nest on the top of it, and ordered that they should not be disturbed. On his return from Alexandria the tent was still standing. "Fostat" is the Arabic word for "tent," and he called his town Fostat, the town of the tent. (Plate I.)

The mosque he built there is the oldest in Cairo. But it has been rebuilt so often, that the present Mosque of Amrou shows few traces of the original structure. (Plate II).

It constantly happens that the earliest remaining monuments of any civilization are already of mature character. The earliest Greek temples date back to about 666 B. C., but they have every mark of being the last of a long series. It is the same with the old Egyptian temples. The earliest examples which remain are obviously a very late product. They also are the last members of a series, the early examples of which have disappeared. So it is here. For two hundred and fifty years after the Hegira the history of Mohammedan architecture is a blank, and what happened can only be guessed. The earliest Egyptian monument which still exists undamaged is the Mosque of Toulun, built in the year 876. (Plate III.)

The Arabs themselves, at least in the beginning, seem to have had little relish for the arts of design, and the development of Mohammedan architecture is apparently due, in the main, to a people of another race. These were the Turks. They, like the Arabs, were a nomadic people, with no art and with even less literature, but they had, as they have shown in many fields, a strenuous disposition, — they were of a masterful turn of mind; they had a sincere appreciation of what was good in the art of design and they had a passion for building. The history of Mohammedan architecture is chiefly the history not of the Arabs' work, nor of work done for the Arabs, but of the work done for the Turks by the races whom they conquered. They made their appearance in Egypt in various guise, as slaves, as mercenaries, as allies, or as conquerors, and in whatever character they appeared they manifested the tyrannical disposition which enabled them to control the government, and the appreciation of art which turns a potentate into a patron. Both ran in their blood.

What is called Saracenic architecture is then, even in Egypt, not that of the Saracens, but that which was patronized by the Turks. Here, as afterwards in Constantinople and in India, they employed native workmen to build and adorn their monuments. But who were these artists? If we knew the history of the first two hundred and fifty years we should be better able to answer this question, but the artists employed in Egypt were apparently the ancient inhabitants of the country, the Copts. The derivation of this name is somewhat disputed. It may come from the town of Coptos, an important Christian city under the Romans. But Copt seems to be "Gypt"; at any rate, the Copts were the old Egyptians. There is another derivation based on the fact that they were Jacobites; "c" "b" "t" spells Copt, very nearly. There was an early Christian father, a Syrian, named Jacob Bar-Dai. He and his followers, called Jacobites, were denounced as heretics by the Council of Calcedon in 415, but the Egyptian Christians held to the Jacobite doctrine, and may possibly have got their name from it. This doctrine, which thus had an oriental rather than a Greek origin, just suited the mystical turn of the Egyptian mind. It held that it was absolutely impossible that in the person of the Saviour the human and the divine should have been united, for the divine cannot possibly have anything in common with the human. This is what is called the Monophysite doctrine,— the theory of only one nature. There are still 600,000 Copts in Egypt who to this day profess the Monophysite heresy. Their religious services are still conducted in the Coptic language, which, however, they no more understand than do most Catholics understand the Latin prayers of their church. If you enter a Coptic church you hear the Coptic language and listen to the last echoes of the ancient Egyptian tongue.

Now these Copts were the artisans and artists whom the Arabians, and afterwards the Turks, employed. It is recorded that the first mosque at Mecca was built by Copts who were captured in the Red Sea, with all their building materials, while on their way to build a church in Abysinnia. By the time of Toulun, in the ninth century, the new style was apparently so perfected that it only needed encouragement to produce works of great splendor. This Toulun was a Turk, one of a band of mercenaries who had been brought from Bagdad. He rose from being steward of the palace to the position of supreme ruler, very much as had happened in France, a hundred years before, when Pepin, Mayor of the Palace, founded the Carlovingian dynasty. Toulun obtained complete control of all Egypt, established the dynasty of the Toulunides and built himself a new mosque at Fostat. Like the mosque of Amrou, which it resembles in plan, it consists mainly of a large court much like the courts of the old Egyptian temples at Luxor and Edfou. (Plate I.)

This central court was called the *Sahn*; the arcades around it, the *Liwan*; the niche showing the direction of Mecca, the *Mihrab* or *Kibleh*; the pulpit, alongside, the *Mimber*; the desk, holding the Koran, the *Kursi*; the gallery or raised platform from which the clerk repeated the lessons was the *Dikkeh*; and the fountain in the middle of the Sahn, the *Sebil*. These features were in time much modified, and some finally disappeared. Under the Baharite Mamelukes the Sahn was much contracted, and the arcades of the Liwan were replaced by great vaulted niches. Finally, in Constantinople the Ottoman Turks covered the Sahn or central court with a dome. Some of the latest and smallest Egyptian mosques, such as the beautiful Bordeni mosque, had only the niche and the pulpit, the Mihrab and the Mimber.

The story told of the mosque of Toulun is that it had been the habit to get columns by pulling down Coptic churches, but that the Coptic architect whom the conqueror wanted to employ refused to have any part in such desecration, and said that if he could have a free hand he would build the finest mosque in the world and not use a single column. This is the mosque of Toulun.

The descendants of Toulun reigned one hundred years. Meanwhile, the heretical Shiites had established themselves in power at Tunis and in the year 970 their general, named Moezz, conquered Egypt and established the dynasty of the Fatimites. This is about the only appearance of the Fatimites in history, except in Persia. These took possession of Fostat and built near by the new town of Cairo. (Plate I.) This was at first a sort of royal suburb. The story here is that they had consulted the astrologers and had strung a string of bells which was to be rung at the propitious moment, giving notice to the workmen to begin work simultaneously. Unfortunately, while they were waiting for their signal a raven passing by lighted on the string, the bells rang and the work was begun, when to their consternation the people found that the planet Mars was just in the ascendant. Mars was considered a planet of evil, but the officers in charge, with much presence of mind, proclaimed that the omen was a happy one, and that the town should be called the victorious. It thus received the name El Kahira, the victorious, from which the modern names of "Le Caire" and "Cairo" are derived.

The years of the Fatimites were among the most splendid in history. Their Cairo was the city of the Arabian Nights. The contemporary and apparently authentic accounts of their display of wealth are almost beyond belief. What remains at this day are only some beautiful private houses and some half ruined mosques, of which the largest is the mosque El Ashar, "the Resplendent" (Plate IV), now used for the University, and the mosque, built by the fanatical Sultan El Hakím, now occupied by the Arabic Museum.

Meanwhile, the Turks were again in evidence, this time as allies. The Seljukian Turks had established themselves in Syria with headquarters at Damascus. The Crusaders undertook to conquer Egypt, and the Fatimite Sultan made an alliance with the Turks at Damascus, who sent Saladin to his assistance, who burned the city of Fostat lest it should fall into the hands of the Crusaders. Its remains are now known as Old Cairo. The modern Cairo consists of the Fatimite suburb El Kahira and the district called Misr, which lies between El Kahira and a Citadel which Saladin built towards the south and by the aid of which, like a Roman of old, he held in subjection the people he had rescued. (Plate I.) Thus the dynasty of Saladin and his descendants replaced the Fatimites. It is called the dynasty of the Ayoubites, from his father, a Seljukian Turk of Damascus named Ayoub. The principal architectural monument of Saladin is this fortress. (Plate IX.)

When, in the year 1250, the Mongols conquered Bagdad, the Abbasside caliphs, as has been said, fled to Egypt and nominally resumed the sway. But they had no political power. The government was seized by successive dynasties of slaves, or Mamelukes. Here again the Turks are in the ascendant, for the first Mamelukes were Turkish. We have met the Turks, first as mercenaries, then as grasping allies. Now they appear as slaves and the Mameluke Sultans of the first dynasty reigned for more than two hundred years. They were called Baharites, being quartered near the Bahr, or river. Two of the most famous mosques were built by them, the Mosque of Sultan Kalahoun (Plate V) and the Mosque of Sultan Hassan (Plate VI). The earlier mosques had been quite plain on the outside, but from the time of the Baharite Mamelukes their buildings began to take on some exterior architectural treatment.

The Mosque of Kalahoun is not merely a mosque. It is also a Muristan, or hospital, and large buildings are connected with it. The Mosque of Sultan Hassan also is really a Medresa, or school, a building ten stories high, attached to which is the tomb of the founder. This is covered by a dome, a construction which was originally used in Egypt only for tombs.

The Turkish Mamelukes were succeeded by a dynasty of Circassian slaves, who are known as the Borghite Mamelukes, or those from the Fort. They built the Mosque of Moayed near the southern gate of the city, much after the plan of the Mosque of Toulun, and splendidly adorned it with marbles. (Plate VIII.) They built also the so-called Tombs of the Caliphs outside the eastern gate, of which the most noticeable are the mosque-tombs of Barqouq (Plate VII) and of Kait Bey (Plate IX). A similar collection of tombs, mostly anonymous, beyond the citadel of Saladin on the south, is called, with better reason, the Tombs of the Mamelukes.

Finally, the Turks appeared in Egypt as conquerors. The Ottomans took Constantinople in 1453, and early in the next century conquered Egypt but continued the Mamelukes in power. Their principal architectural works are the mosques at Broussa in Bithynia and those built in Constantinople in imitation of the church of St. Sophia. About a hundred years ago the Egyptian ruler Mehemet Ali murdered all the Mamelukes within the Citadel of Saladin and built there a mosque after the Constantinople pattern. (Plate IX.)

Meanwhile, although the Mameluke governors had not done very much building in Cairo, two of their mosques are of special interest, — the mosque at Boulak, a suburb of Cairo near the river (Plate X), and the little Bordeni mosque, near the Citadel (Plate X). The Boulak mosque, and a copy of it within the precincts of the University, is covered with a dome, but it is in plan and arrangement entirely unlike the domed mosques at Constantinople, and both in design and in architectural treatment it is one of the most original and charming of buildings. The Bordeni mosque, built about seventy years later, is very beautiful in detail, but without structural features. It is merely an oblong room with a niche and a pulpit, the Mihrab and Mimber, but no Sahn; that is to say, no court.

II.

But the quality of Mohammedan architecture lies not wholly in the disposition of the plans and the composition of the masses within and without. The novelty, ingenuity and elegance of the structural and decorative details are equally admirable, and some of them present peculiarities of unusual interest.

The most conspicuous of these is the so-called honeycomb, or stalactite, work, a singular device which is used on the under-side of all sorts of projections, almost to the exclusion of mouldings. Capitals, cornices, string-courses, brackets, arches and vaults, domes and the pendentives that support them, are entirely composed of little niches piled one above another in an endless variety of fantastic combinations. Sometimes these are rectilinear, and resemble a broken honeycomb; sometimes they are bounded by curved surfaces. It is not difficult to devise theories as to the origin of this unique feature. But since for the first two hundred and fifty years after the Hegira we have no Mohammedan buildings, and in the oldest that now survive the distinctive features of the style are, as has been said, already fully formed, all hypotheses in regard to its source are equally difficult of verification. Everybody is free to choose for himself the one that seems to him to be the most reasonable.

1. From a strictly historical point of view, the most interesting theory is that which finds the first suggestion of stalactites in what are apparently the earliest known Mohammedan buildings, the so-called tombs of Zobeide and of Ezekiel, near Bagdad, built by Haroun al Raschid about the year 810. These tombs are roofed over by successive ranges of overhanging brick niches, in ten or twelve stories, each niche being supported upon corbels, which in the tomb of Zobeide occupy the spandrels between the niches; in the tomb of Ezekiel, which seems to be a later development, they rest upon their summits. Both treatments are to be found in stalactite work. The interior of these tombs, if covered with a coat of stucco, would present very much the aspect of a stalactite dome. (Plate XI.)

2. One theory finds in stalactites an imitation in miniature of a form of domical construction still used in Persia. These domes are formed by a series of interlacing arches which leave between them diamond shaped panels, which in many examples are scooped out in the form of shells. The effect is not unlike some of the larger honeycomb domes of Egypt, one of which is illustrated in Plate XIII. But no historical connection between the two has been clearly made out.

For these suggestions I am indebted to a paper read before the Royal Institute of British Architects by my friend Mr. Spiers in April, 1888.

3. One might, however, if he were to disregard these intimations, fancy that the pile of niches, or small domes, which constitute the simplest and presumably the earliest variety of stalactite work, were an imitation, *in petto*, of the pile of great half-domes and niches to be found at the eastern end of the church of St. Sophia at Constantinople. (Plate XI.)

The imitation upon a small scale, for solely decorative purposes, of large constructive features, — such as columns, capitals and entablatures, arches and arcades, piers, brackets and pediments, — is of frequent occurrence in all styles of architecture, and for a century before the Hegira these great niches and the spherical pendentives upon which they rest had been the wonder of the world as much for their grace and beauty as for their dignity and boldness. What more likely, then, than that they should be decoratively reproduced on a smaller scale? But in point of fact this seems not to have happened, even in the countries most directly under the influence of Byzantine art. It was not likely to happen in Egypt, for the Copts, in their art as well as in their religion, sedulously repelled all Greek influences, and the Byzantine dome with its pendentives played in fact little part in Mohammedan architecture until, a thousand years later, Constantinople was taken by the Turks. In Egypt, as afterwards in Persia and Hindostan, the transition from a square plan below to a circular dome above, or from a rectangular recess to the semicircular niche which covers it, is generally made by throwing arches across the corners, thus bringing the square to an octagon. The spandrels between the arches are not occupied by hollow spherical surfaces, as at St. Sophia, but are sometimes left plain, and sometimes filled with great polygonal or even star-shaped brackets. It is in this feature, not in the Byzantine half-domes, that we may perhaps find the prototypes of the little stalactite niches and of the corbels sometimes which support them. Examples of this are shown in Plate XI.

That from the Fayoum shows the inside of a dome of cut stone which passes from the square below to the circle above by way of eight-sided and sixteen-sided polygons. In the smaller one from the Tombs of the Caliphs, the arch thrown across the corner of the square is filled in with four rows of little niches which, with the broken spandrels between them, almost exactly reproduce in miniature the larger construction above. In this example the overhanging piers between the upper niches do not come in line with the piers below, the re-entering angle between the spandrels being ill-calculated to support them, but, as in the Tomb of Ezekiel, they rest upon the crowns of the niches, which are thrown forward to receive them.

In the larger one, however, of the niches form Cairo doorways, the spandrel is occupied with an octagonal, or even star-shaped, corbel, which also is reproduced in miniature between the niches of the stalactite work which fills the upper arch, to support the little piers that separate the niches. These may well have been suggested by the large ones below. The smaller niche also shows these star-shaped corbels.

It is to be noticed that these great corbels closely resemble the inverted polygonal and star-shaped pyramids which occur in some later developments of Gothic groining, though they lack the ribs which are the characteristic element in Gothic vaulting. The cusped and pointed arches, also, remind one of mediæval work. But this elaborate and beautiful development of Saracenic groining seems, curiously enough, to have been confined to these doorways, and not to have been used for the vaulting of interiors, which was probably considered too bold an undertaking.

The larger example from the Tombs of the Caliphs shows how rows of niches were made to take the shape and exactly fulfil the function of a Byzantine pendentive.

It was, moreover, a peculiarity of the Saracenic builders that, with a singular neglect of constructive propriety in design, they habitually left the arches which were thus thrown across the corners hanging in the air, without any supporting corbels at all, as may be seen in the example from the Fayoum. The constant recurrence of this curious treatment in the miniature stalactite niches, as is exemplified in the other domes, would seem to confirm the hypothesis that they owe their origin to the imitation of larger constructive members.

4. But it is hardly necessary to go so far afield as Persia or Bagdad, or even to suppose that stalactite work is the imitation in miniature of larger constructions nearer home, since the methods of brick building now used in Egypt offer forms closely analogous to them and of the same diminutive scale. The brick corbels habitually employed in modern construction look very much like the angular, or honeycomb, variety of stalactites, and they need only to be covered with a coat of plaster,

as walls in Egypt have always been covered, to produce what the Spaniards call the egg-shell variety, the plaster filling up and rounding off the sharpness of the angles. The four figures on the bottom of Plate XI illustrate this suggestion.

How much credence should be given to either of these hypotheses must depend upon the support afforded them by the facts of history, data which seem to be at present inaccessible. Without such support the most plausible and self-consistent theories are of little worth. But these inquiries are after all merely a matter of curiosity; for what gives vogue to manners and customs is the vital thing, not what starts them. The women now march off in a body at the end of a dinner, deserting the men, in order that each party may, for a change, consort for a while with their own kind, not, as in the origin of the custom, because the society of gentlemen in their cups is liable to become uncongenial to ladies. So here, and in the contemporary Gothic architecture, the important question is, not what first suggested stalactites and pointed arches, but why these varieties, or species, once planted, suddenly overran their respective fields, to the exclusion and suppression of other forms, with all the tyranny of a dominant fashion.

It is not so important to know what was the first hint of stalactites, as to know why the suggestion was taken up and developed with so much zeal. This seems to have been due to a predilection for geometrical ornament, and this, in turn, to have been due to the mystical turn of mind of the later Egyptians. A repugnance to the use of the human form, and even of the forms of animal and vegetable nature, was an eminently Coptic prepossession. The Mohammedan precept forbidding painting and sculpture is not found in the Koran, but the successors of Mahomet, in their exposition of the Koran, seem to have adopted the idea from the Copts, wishing probably to make converts among them. The Koran says one shall not *worship* the image of anything created, but the Copts went further and objected to making any representations of any created thing. This is now the teaching of the orthodox Mohammedans in nearly the entire Mohammedan world, although the heretical Fatimites, both during their ascendancy in Cairo and nowadays in Persia, have largely rejected it.

The Copts were ascetics. It was in the Egyptian mountains that the solitary life of the first hermits was established. In their distrust of the natural world and its beguiling beauties they even went so far as to consider that curved lines were of the evil one. No right minded person would tolerate anything but right lines, and in their architecture the Coptic builders even revived the rectilinear arches which are found in the earliest Egyptian pyramids. In the decorative work of the Mohammedans, accordingly, the lines are nearly all straight and the few curved lines which are employed represent only geometrical figures. These predispositions had already been conspicuously manifested in the time of the Romans, who called the mosaics which were made up of square and triangular tesserae, carefully shaped and fitted, by the name of *Opus Alexandrinum*. Extraordinary skill and invention are shown also in the construction of interlacing patterns, and in the inlaying of marbles or other stones, often making the inlaid figure and the background of the same shape but reversed. The skill thus fostered found abundant exercise in developing all the possibilities of stalactite work, which by the time of its first appearance in existing buildings had attained an intricacy and complexity which well nigh baffles comprehension, and as we have seen, makes it almost impossible to tell in what structural suggestions it may have originated. In despair of finding any rational explanations, some writers have even turned to symbolism and fancied that the little niches of which the work is made up of are repetitions on a smaller scale of the Mihrab, or sacred niche, which in every mosque points the worshipper's face towards Mecca.

In view of all this we may not be far wrong if we take the view that, these accumulations of hollow niches having once commended themselves to the taste of the time, the same patient ingenuity and exuberant fancy which led to the elaboration of geometrical patterns in the flat, found in the problems of solid geometry which these studies presented, an equally congenial field. And just as in their patterns of wood and marble inlays and interlacings, forms suggested by weaving and bricklaying, they adhered to the straight lines and circles which geometry affords, so here they enriched their cylinders, hemispheres, and parallelopipedons by adding to them whatever suggestions were offered by the groinings and corbellings of the stonemason and brick-layer, thus giving a new interest to their work. One may as well suppose these to be the last steps in the process of development as the first.

A less well-known example of their geometrical ingenuity is their solution of the problem of architecturally squaring the circle, so to speak; that is, of connecting a square figure with a circular one. This problem found its most famous solution in the pendentive dome of St. Sophia. The transition is there made by means of spherical triangles, and the Romanesque architects adopted the same device not only in their domes but, on a smaller scale, in making the transition from a round shaft to a square abacus or plinth, in the so-called "cushion" capitals and bases. But the geometrical Copts hit upon another device which was exceptionally clever and which better suited their rectilinear turn of mind. Knowing that between any three points a plane triangular surface may be drawn, they took any number of points on the circle and from these points passed zig-zag lines connecting them with an equal number of points upon the square. The surface connecting the square and the circle was thus divided into plane triangles, each of which was sometimes broken up into three smaller triangles by depressing a point in its centre; and these again sometimes given a similar treatment. Examples of this device are found in the base of the columns which flank the great doorway of the Mosque of Sultan Hassan, and in the base of the minarets of the mosque at Boulak and of the Suleimanieh at Constantinople. Several capitals in Cairo and those in the porch of the Mosque of Rustem Pasha, also in Constantinople, exemplify the same method. My friend Mr. Partridge has furnished me with a curious example of the same thing from the church of St. Remi at Rheims. (Plate XII).

The same device is employed on the outside of the Tombs of

the Caliphs and of the Mamelukes at Cairo, to pass from the square walls below to the base of the circular or polygonal dome above. An elaborate series of large mouldings, like a gigantic chamfer-stop, was also adopted in these buildings to give to the exterior surface of the pendentives an appropriate architectural treatment, a problem which both the Gothic and the Renaissance architects have constantly evaded. (Plate XII.)

The most interesting application of this expedient is to be found, however, not in Constantinople or in Cairo, but at Broussa, where the Ottoman Turks established themselves, as has been said, before crossing into Europe. In the domes of several of the mosques, and in a great niche, a half-dome, at the entrance to one of them, the transition from the square below to the circle above is effected in this manner. (Plate XII.) One of the examples shows each of the original triangles occupied by nine smaller ones. I do not know that these buildings have yet been published, or that attention has been called to these clever geometrical constructions.

Other distinctive devices of the Mohammedans are the horseshoe arch and dome, and the domes supported upon intersecting arches which are to be found in Sicily, Spain, India, and Persia. But any discussion of these, or of the more purely decorative methods of the Mohammedans, would take more space and time than are now at our command.

THE MOSQUE OF AMROU, A.D., 642.

PLATE III.

THE MOSQUE OF TOULUN, A. D. 876.

THE MOSQUE EL AŠHAR (THE UNIVERSITY) A. D., 981.

PLATE V.

THE MOSQUE OF SULTAN KALAHOUN, A. D., 1287.

THE MOSQUE SULTAN HASSAN, A. D., 1377.

PLATE VII.

THE MOSQUE OF BARQUOQ, A. D., 1382.

PLATE VIII.

THE MOSQUE OF MOAYED, A. D., 1412.

THE MOSQUE OF KAIT-BEY, A. D., 1463.

THE CITADEL OF SALADIN, A. D., 1166.
THE MOSQUE OF MEHEMET ALI, A. D., 1815.

PLATE X.

THE MOSQUE OF BOULAK, A. D., 1571.

THE BORDENI MOSQUE, A. D., 1638.

PLATE XI.

STALACTITES.

PLATE XII.

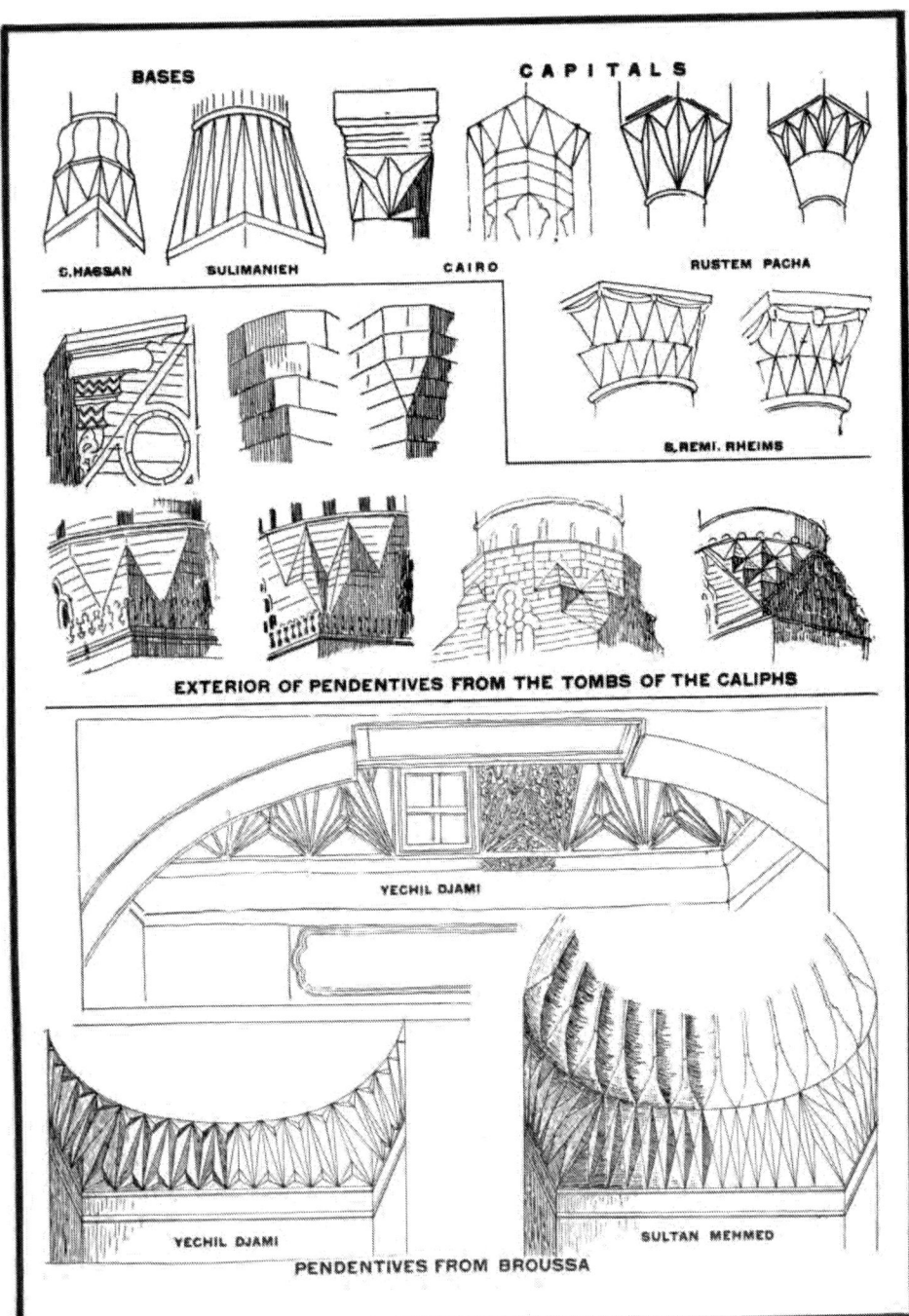

ZIGZAGS.

DOME OF THE MOSQUE OF MOHAMMED BEY, CAIRO, A.D., 1774.

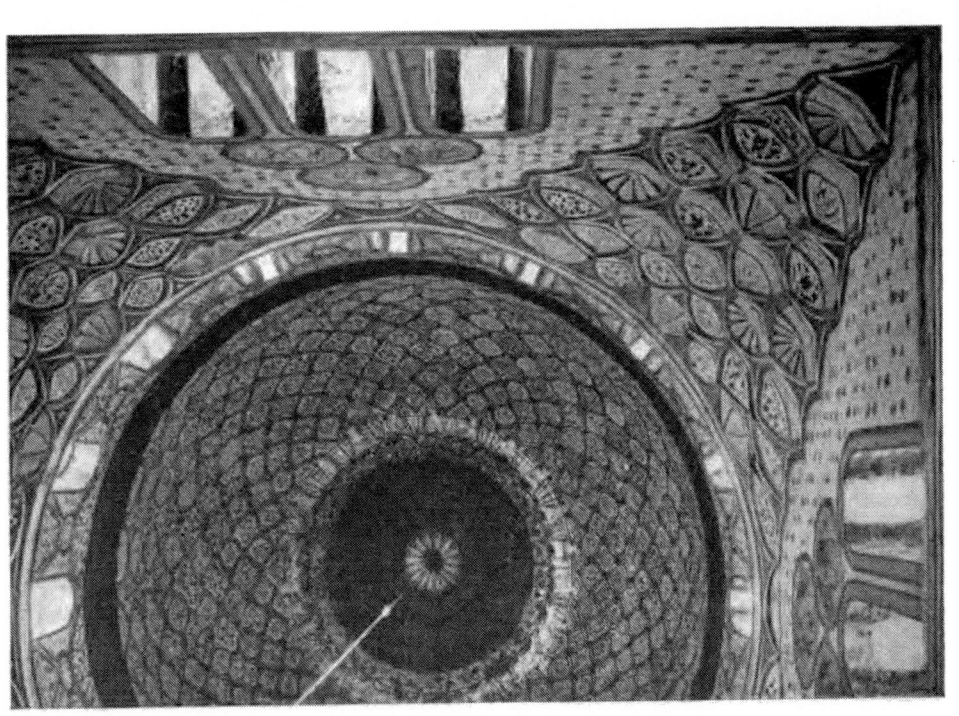

DOORWAY OF THE MOSQUE OF SULTAN MEHMED, BROUSSA, A.D., 1389.

Printed by Libri Plureos GmbH in Hamburg,
Germany